Roary

Roary is an English single-seater racing car. His engine is at the back and drives his back wheels round to push him along.

Front suspension

Front wing

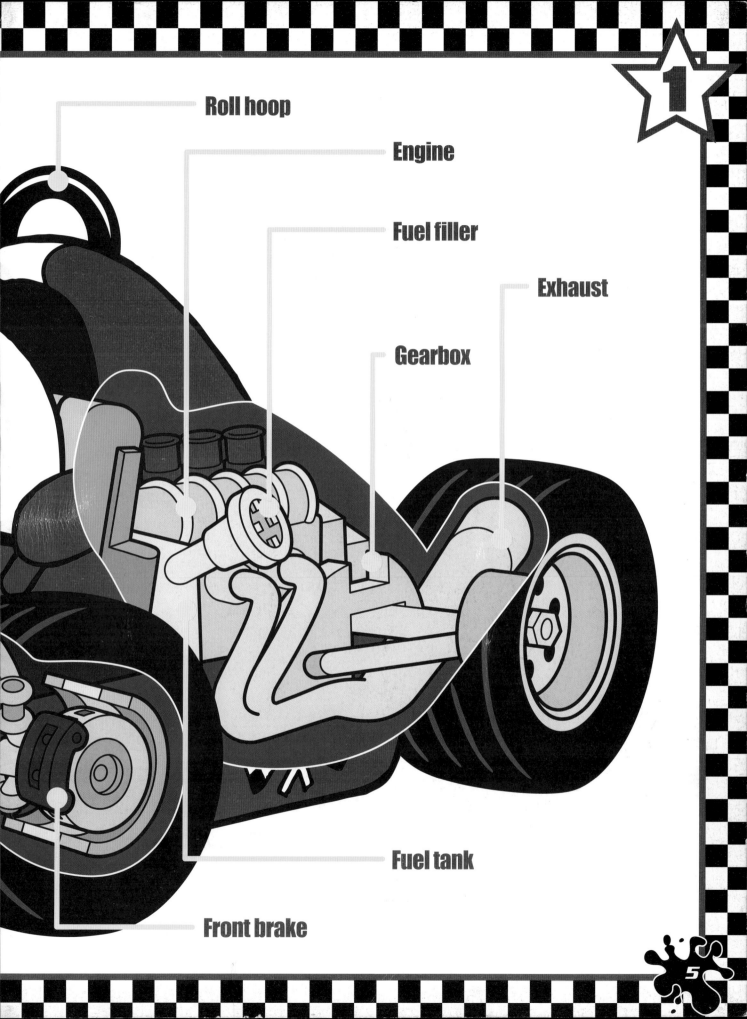

Roll hoop

Engine

Fuel filler

Exhaust

Gearbox

Fuel tank

Front brake

Silver Hatch racetrack

Ton-Up Tunnel

Silver Hatch Farm

Dinkie's Corner

Rally Track

Tummy Turn Bridge

Hare-Pin Bend

Workshop

Starting Grid

Marsha's Marshall Post

Racing with Roary

➡ Starting grid

The cars line up on the starting grid ready for the race. The red starting lights come on one by one, and when they all go out, the cars zoom off.

⬅ Racing

Roary and Maxi race each other round the track, with the other cars close behind.

3

← Brake and zoom

The cars use their brakes to slow down for Hare-Pin Bend, then they rev their engines to zoom out of the corner. Their grippy tyres help them to stick to the track.

⮕ Too fast

If Roary goes too fast through the corners, he slides across the track. Sliding is fun and makes Roary laugh, but it slows him down and the other cars begin to catch him up.

4

5

← The finish line

Marsha waves the chequered flag as Roary crosses the finish line to win the race, with Maxi right behind him. Everyone cheers for Roary, Silver Hatch's No.1 star!

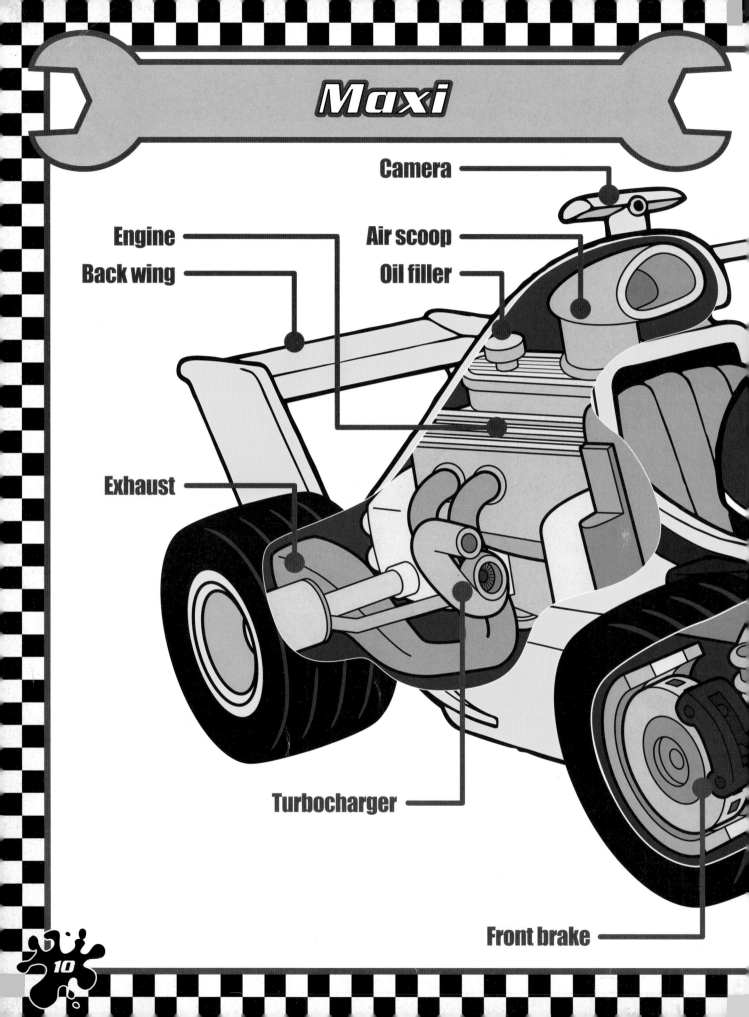

Maxi

Camera

Engine

Back wing

Air scoop

Oil filler

Exhaust

Turbocharger

Front brake

10

Maxi is a fast Italian F1 single-seater racing car. He has front and back wings to push him down onto the track and to help him zoom through corners.

Front suspension

Front wing

➡ Gearbox

Roary's engine powers a gearbox to turn his back wheels round and push him along.

⬅ Exhaust

Roary has exhaust pipes to get rid of the dirty gasses from his engine.

➡ Brake lights

Drifter's brake lights glow when he uses his brakes to slow down.

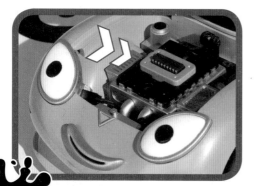

⬅ Computer

Drifter has an on-board computer to control his go-faster gadgets.

⬆ Air filter

Tin Top has an air filter to stop dust in the air damaging his engine.

⬇ Air scoop

Maxi's air scoop sucks in air to mix with his fuel and give his engine lots of power.

⬆ Oil filler

Big Chris uses the oil filler on Maxi's engine to fill him with oil.

⬅ Flip-ups

Maxi has flip-ups to make the air flow over his back wheels.

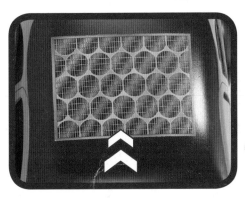

⬆ Solar panel

Cici's solar panel charges her battery using light from the sun.

⬅ Battery

Cici's special solar battery can power her along instead of her engine.

Silver Hatch workshop

Lets find out what happens inside Silver Hatch workshop

▶ Manuals

Silver Hatch workshop is where Big Chris looks after the cars. His manuals show him how to fix any tricky problems.

🔺 Oil

Big Chris uses his oil can to fix squeaks, and oil helps moving parts to run smoothly.

🔺 Tools

Big Chris uses wrenches, screwdrivers and spanners when he works on the cars.

Toolbox

All Big Chris's important tools are kept in his tool box so that he can find them easily.

Big Chris

Big Chris loves to be in the workshop looking after the cars – he's a Motor Man!

Cici

Cici is a little French stunt car. She can use her engine or a special solar battery to power her along.

Charging socket

Back suspension

Back brake

Front suspension

Front brake

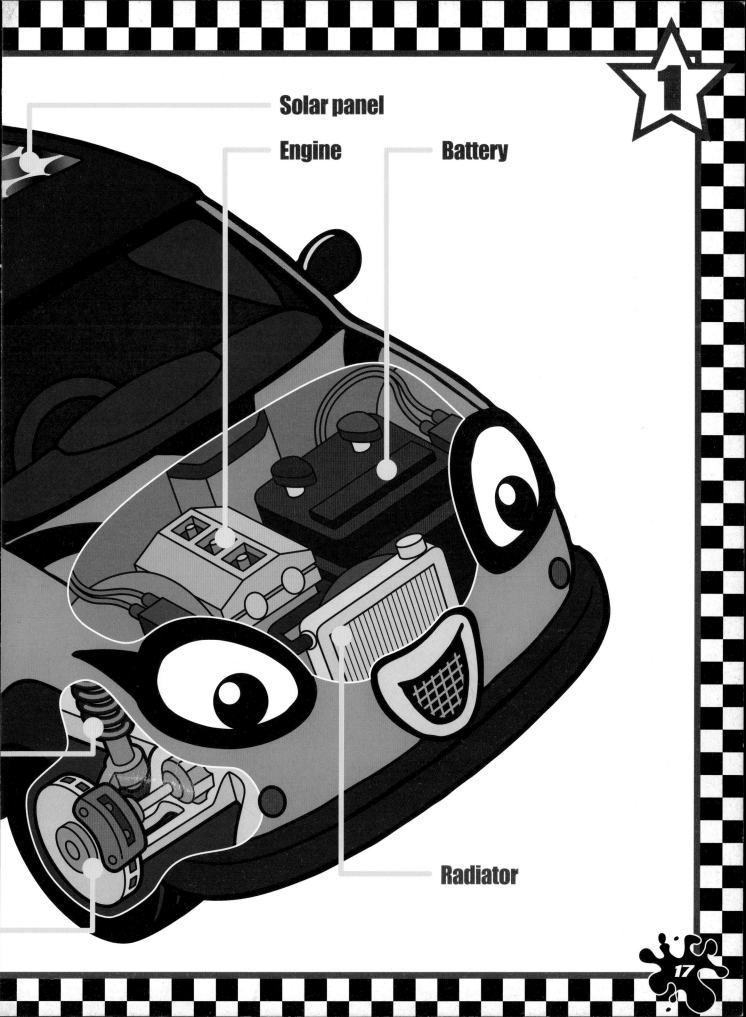

Solar panel

Engine

Battery

Radiator

Looking after Roary

1 After each race, Big Chris checks Roary's engine, changes his oil and makes sure he's ready for the next race.

2 Roary's engine can run on ordinary fuel or Farmer Green's bio-fuel. Big Chris uses a fuel pump to fill Roary's tank.

3 If Roary has a flat tyre, Big Chris has to change his wheel. He uses a jack to lift him up, and an air-wrench to unscrew his wheel nut. With a new wheel fitted, Roary's ready to go.

4 Big Chris washes Roary after each race and gives him a polish to keep his red paintwork clean and shiny.

Marsha's flags

▲ Marsha

Marsha waves her flags to signal to the cars when they're racing out on the track. Each different coloured flag has a special meaning.

▲ Danger

The yellow flag warns the cars to slow down because there's danger on the track.

🚧 Stop
The red flag tells the cars to stop racing and drive slowly back to the pits.

🚧 Safe
The green flag means the danger has passed and it's safe to race again.

🚧 Behave
The black and white flag warns the cars to behave and stop being naughty.

🚧 Winner
The chequered flag is waved as the winning car crosses the finish line to win the race.

Drifter

Drifter is a high-tech Japanese street car. He has an on-board computer to control his go-faster gadgets.

On-board computer

Engine

Radiator

Front brake

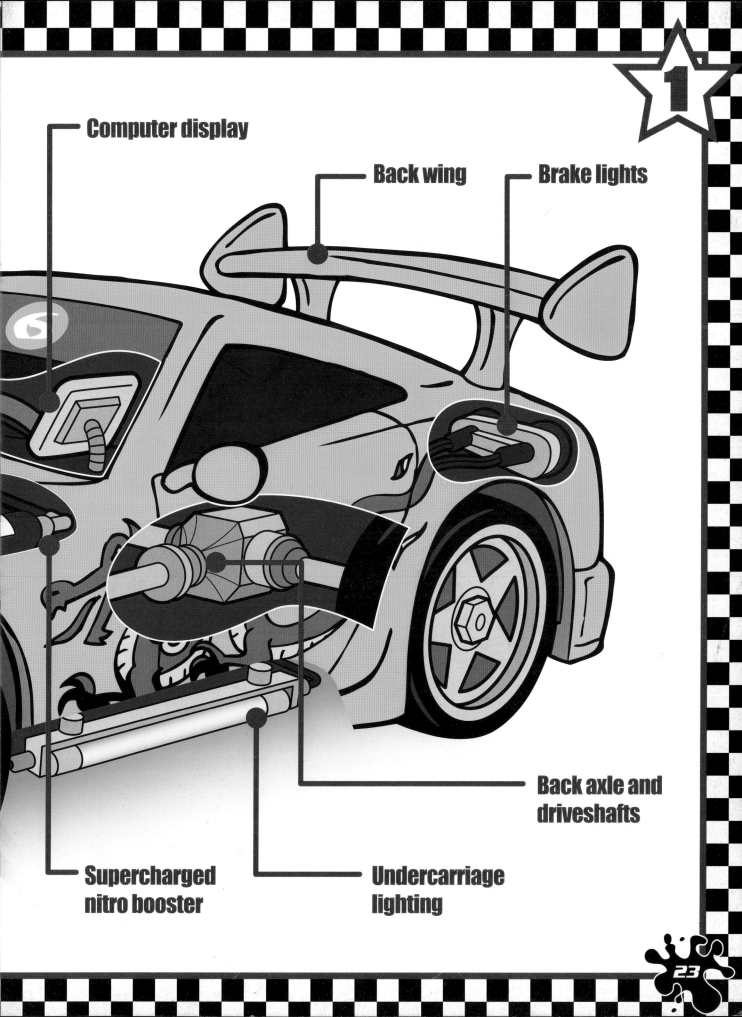

Computer display

Back wing

Brake lights

Back axle and
driveshafts

Supercharged
nitro booster

Undercarriage
lighting

Roary's friends

FB *is Farmer Green's truck. He delivers things to the race track.*

Plugger *is the Silver Hatch rescue 4x4. He's very cool.*

Zippee *is Marsha's scooter. She likes to zip around.*

Conrod *is an Australian V8 Supercar. He loves to visit Silver Hatch to see his pals.*

Loada *carries the cars when they travel away from the track.*

Nick *the* Police car wishes he could race round the track.

Hellie *is* Mr. Carburettor's helicopter. He lands on the roof of the workshop.

Rusty is Big Chris's caravan. He likes sleeping.

Breeze *lives* on the beach. She loves driving on the sand.

James *is* Mama Mia's car. He has lots of gadgets to show off.

1

Mr. Carburettor's team

Big Chris *looks after all the cars.*

Marsha *organises the track and races.*

Mama Mia *is Mr. Carburettor's mum.*

Big Christine *is Big Chris's mum.*

PC Pete *makes sure the cars are safe.*

Farmer Green *makes bio-fuel for the cars.*

Mr. Carburettor owns Silver Hatch racetrack. He often visits to see the cars and watch them race.

Flash likes to play tricks on the cars.

Dinkie lives next to the track.

Molecom helps out around the track.

Tin Top

Tin Top is a big American saloon car. He's very strong, but is always getting bumped and bashed.

Air filter

Engine

Air vent

Radiator

Front suspension

Roll cage

Back wing

Back axle and driveshafts

Front brake

Roary's racing facts

1 Roary is the youngest car at Silver Hatch. He likes to spin his wheels and shout "Light 'em up".

4 Drifter has a supercharged nitro booster. He can use it to overtake the other cars.

2 Maxi is the fastest, loudest and most expensive car at Silver Hatch racetrack.

5 Cici is the smallest car at Silver Hatch. She loves to drive fast and do stunts and tricks.

3 Tin Top is very ticklish and laughs whenever Big Chris repairs his dented panels.

6 Plugger has a music system that plays through his special loudspeaker mirrors.